THE GALE & POLDEN TRAINING SERIES

DEFENCE OF VILLAGES AND SMALL TOWNS

By
COLONEL G. A. WADE, M.C.

AUTHOR OF
" The Defence of Bloodford Village," etc.

The Naval & Military Press Ltd

Published by

The Naval & Military Press Ltd
Unit 5 Riverside, Brambleside
Bellbrook Industrial Estate
Uckfield, East Sussex
TN22 1QQ England

Tel: +44 (0)1825 749494

www.naval-military-press.com
www.nmarchive.com

SUMMARY

WANTED: A SENSE OF REALITY.
>Shed your rosy delusions.

STRATEGIC IMPORTANCE OF VILLAGES.
>Defence in **depth.**
>**Strongholds** across enemy's path.
>If spirited defence Germans may **give it a miss.**

WHAT KIND OF ATTACK?
>Small number stealthily?
>Great force?

OPPOSE FORCE WITH FORCE.
>Do not dissipate strength.

WHICH PARTS VITAL TO DEFEND?
>Bridge—Reservoir—Police station—A.R.P. control—Transformer.

NEED FOR RESERVE.
>To **hit back** with.
>To **restore situation.**
>To **reinforce.**

SITING THE KEEPS.
>All-round defence—Covering vital parts—Mutually supporting.
>No. 1.—The Brickworks.
>No. 2.—Reservoir Hill.
>No. 3.—Gardens, DOWNIT ROAD.
>No. 4.—Old Water Mill.
>No. 5.—Market Hall.

DESCRIPTION OF KEEPS.
>No. 2.—**Wiring** in hedges and trees. Northover projectors on near slope covering three roads.
>Screens, dummy mines, bombers' trenches.
>No. 3.—**House** included—wiring not visible from **air.**
>Dig parts of trenches now.
>Clear field of fire (**discrimination**).

ROAD BLOCKS.

      Challenge to the enemy.

      Easy to defend—**Hard** to attack.

      Surprise—take advantage of it.

      What will enemy do?

      Road Block A.—South of Gasworks.

      Road Block B.—Blocks UPPIT Road.

      Road Block C.—DOWNIT Road. No. 3 Keep mans it.

      Road Block D.—BEATIT Road Bridge—high crown.

      In addition, two **Light Road Blocks.**

      Road Block E.—Near drive to Hall.

      Road Block F.—WEST CORNER of Graveyard.

FRAMEWORK OF DEFENCE NOW COMPLETE.

THE FIGHTING PATROLS.

      Divide district into patrol areas.

      Well-marked boundaries.

      Cyclist patrol—silent—quick.

MEN AND WEAPONS.

      150 Men.

      80 Rifles—20 shot-guns—4 Brownings.

      6 Tommy-guns—2 Northovers—2 flame-throwers.

      Bombs, anti-tank mines, etc.

      Men.

        60 Men to garrison keeps.

        50 Men for two fighting patrols.

        15 Men for road blocks.

        25 Men for reserve.

      Weapons.

      Brownings in Keeps Nos. 1, 2, 3, 4.

      Tommy-guns: 2 to fighting patrols, 4 in Keep No. 5.

      Northovers: No. 2 Keep.

      Flame-throwers: B road block.

      Anti-tank mines: road blocks E and F.

HOW WILL OUR DEFENCES WORK?

      Picture **attack.**

3

ROUNDING OFF THE DEFENCE SCHEME.
> Time factor.
> " Fight on! "

LIAISON.
> Neighbouring units.
> Council—Police—A.R.P. (wounded)—W.V.S.
> Electricity—Gas—Water—Food.
> Petrol disruption.

BLOCK LANDING GROUNDS.

BARBED WIRE.
> Photography.

COMMUNICATIONS.
> Flag and lamp.

TANK TRAPS.

WATER IN DEFENCE.
> Dam.
> Boat patrols.

SHOT-GUNS.
> Buckshot.

TRAINING.
> Fighting patrols (endless interest).
> House-to-house fighting.
> Shooting—close range—darkness.

CHRONOLOGICAL DEFENCE IN DEPTH.
> **" Splash! "**
> Stores of weapons, etc.

SAY " WHAT WILL HE DO? " " HOW WILL HE DO IT? " ANSWERS WILL NEVER FAIL TO GIVE YOU THE CLUE TO A **SUCCESSFUL DEFENCE.**

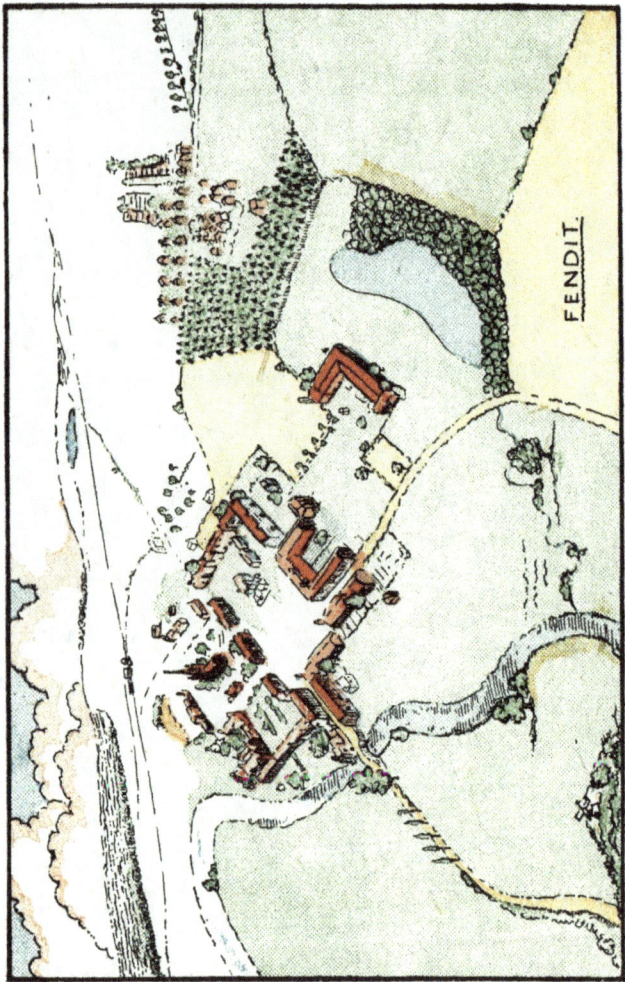

PLATE 1.—VIEW OF FENDIT

DEFENCE OF VILLAGES AND SMALL TOWNS

I

WANTED : A SENSE OF REALITY

Up to a year or so ago none of us could imagine our beautiful English villages, the picture of peace and contentment, being attacked by anything more deadly than charabancs and sightseers.

Yet here we are, faced with not only the possibility but the *probability* of having to defend them against invaders, heavily armed, scientifically trained and treacherous.

When I first began to study the defence of the villages which I had known and loved since boyhood, I discovered that I was suffering from some sort of vague handicap, some feeling which hindered me in doing justice to the job, something which prevented my taking that depth of interest which the subject warranted.

Thinking the matter over I finally made an absolutely astounding discovery—it was simply this: I was not putting my heart into the defence schemes for these places simply because they were so familiar and I loved them so much that I could not bring myself to believe that anything could threaten their existence! Somehow I could not picture them as the centre of bloodshed, devastation and death.

In other words, I could not go all out on the defence schemes because I was not convinced that they would ever be necessary!

Not to put too fine a point on it, I was being just exactly the sort of b.f. Hitler has banked on my being —unable to realize the threat until too late!

After that I did some hard thinking which caused me to shed my rosy delusions, and I want you to do the same before I go on to talk about village defence.

Do not, any of you, listen to me with the same sort of casual detachment with which you hear the preacher describing the perils you are storing up for yourselves in the hereafter, because to-day we are NOT dealing with the remote future but with the next few months, and *above all things* we must immediately develop a SENSE OF REALITY.

Now I am going to assume that YOU have just been charged with the responsibility of defending the village of FENDIT with your company of Home Guard, and we will discuss the problem together.

II

STRATEGIC IMPORTANCE OF VILLAGE DEFENCE

Nowadays we hear a lot about defence in depth, and nobody likes to talk about " holding the line."

The Germans have become accustomed to staging mobile heavily armed attacks, and against these only defence in depth is of any use.

If you picture the onslaught of the Panzer division as like the impact of a bullet, then loose, clinging resistance is like the sand in the sandbag which will stop it in a much shorter distance than other substances offering considerably harder resistance.

When the invader bursts into our countryside those who are defending our villages will have a role of absolutely primary importance. Every centre of resistance the enemy meets will slow him down and use up a little of his impetus. If these strongholds are distributed right across his path, as villages will be, before he has travelled far his pace will be slowed, his initiative gone and the way prepared for action by our own shock troops.

Another aspect of village defence is this: the Germans are trained not to break their heads on tough spots but to by-pass well-defended localities, so that, even although the enemy may be present in overwhelming force, if the village puts up a spirited resistance he will probably give it a miss. But before doing so he will test the defences in a most determined way, and the village will not be held unless it has a GOOD DEFENCE SCHEME well co-ordinated and carried out.

The preparation of this scheme is *your* responsibility, so make it a good one.

GENERAL CONSIDERATIONS

The first step is to consider what kind of attack it is that we have to guard against.

It may be that at sunset or dawn a comparatively small number of Huns will drop from the skies, stealthily and speedily assemble and attack the village, or it may be that one day the sounds of battle will be heard in the far distance and the enemy, in great force, preceded by armoured fighting vehicles, will come moving across the landscape.

We do not know HOW he will come, but we *do* know that when he *does* come our village must be ready for him.

Consequently, we must have our dispositions such that we can not only hunt and exterminate small bodies of Germans, but, if attacked by larger numbers, can oppose force with force and surprise them by delivering a heavy counter-attack.

Now you can only meet force with force if you have been sufficiently strong-willed to withstand the great temptation which is always present when making defensive plans—I mean the tendency to dissipate your strength in a host of small unco-ordinated posts so spread out all over the place that a compact body of the enemy could mop up five or six times their own number by taking them a few at a time.

Admittedly every one of those small posts would be guarding something useful, and if you take them away you will feel you are giving something to the enemy without a fight. But that is the price you have to pay for your ability to strike back at the Hun, and, believe me, you will find it well worth while, particularly if you make a careful study of what you are giving away so that you let the enemy have nothing that is really vital.

In any case, when we come to discuss fighting patrols you will see that even though no posts are stationed in a particular area it does not by any means follow that Germans can safely enter.

Now let us look at the village to make up our minds which parts it is vital to defend and which parts are such that if the enemy occupies them it will not be disastrous.

9

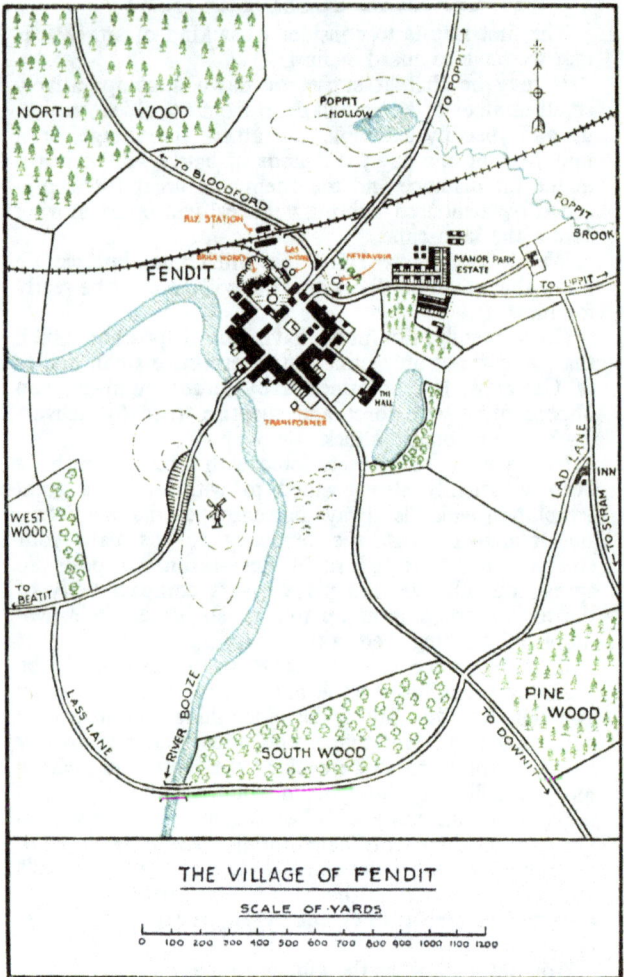

THE VILLAGE OF FENDIT

SCALE OF YARDS

0 100 200 300 400 500 600 700 800 900 1000 1100 1200

PLATE 2.—MAP OF FENDIT

10

(1) The RIVER BOOZE is considerable protection against attack from the SOUTH-WEST, so the BRIDGE must be strongly held.

(2) Damage to the PUMPING STATION or RESER-VOIR would be a serious matter, and, in addition, an enemy on RESERVOIR HILL could dominate the defences.

(3) The COUNCIL OFFICES, POLICE HEAD-QUARTERS, A.R.P. CONTROL are all in the heart of the village, so they will be all right, but the TRANSFORMER STATION is rather isolated on the SOUTH.

These places I have mentioned must all be protected within your scheme.

On the other hand, although if plenty of men were available it would be desirable to hold the RAILWAY STATION, MANOR PARK ESTATE and THE HALL, they are all places which the enemy could occupy without seriously threatening the main part of the village; consequently, to avoid too wide dispersion, they will not be defended by posts.

This will mean that three points will arise:—

(1) The members of the Home Guard who live on Manor Park Estate will have a meeting and say they want *their* houses embraced within the main defences and that they joined the Home Guard to defend their own homes and not other people's.

(2) The Squire will raise hell and say you do not know your business and that if the chaps he served with in the South African War were here they would soon teach you that the Hall should be the *centre* of the defence.

After you have pacified the Squire and the Manor Park Estate worthies by a dissertation on the deadly effectiveness of the fighting patrols with which you intend to cover their respective areas, you come to the third point, which is the one which really matters.

(3) You will have some MEN IN RESERVE, men to hit back with, men to restore the situation if it gets critical, men to reinforce the threatened parts.

IV

SITING THE KEEPS

We will start with our KEEPS; the strongholds which will have garrisons to defend them to the bitter end and from which our fighting patrols and reserves can sally forth for ACTIVE DEFENCE farther afield.

As far as possible the keeps should:

    (i) Be capable of ALL-ROUND DEFENCE.

    (ii) Be sited where they cover approaches to vital parts.

    (iii) Be mutually supporting.

Good places for keeps will be:—

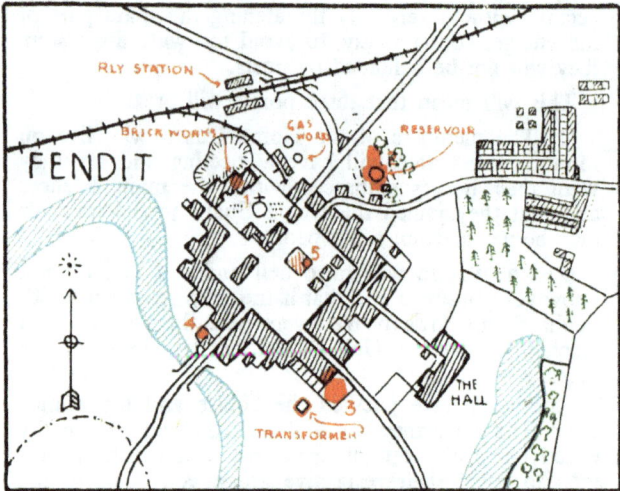

PLATE 3.—KEEPS

12

No. **1 Keep** at the BRICKWORKS. This will be protected on the NORTH by the clay pit. The building is robust and the kiln, being of tremendously thick brickwork, will make an admirable shelter. From this keep the gasworks can be protected from attack coming from the railway station, and there is visual contact with No. 2 Keep on Reservoir Hill. The churchyard on the south gives an open field of fire and will be very handy for the disposal of attackers.

No. **2 Keep** on RESERVOIR HILL will take advantage of the natural cover furnished by the trees and commands the three roads from BLOODFORD, POPPIT and UPPIT as well as guarding the east of the gasworks.

No. **3 Keep** in the ALLOTMENT GARDENS will cover the DOWNIT ROAD. It also protects the transformer station and is in visual contact with the Bridge Keep (No. 4).

No. **4 Keep** will be the OLD WATER MILL near the BRIDGE. It has a good field of fire across the river, and the garrison can reach the road block on the bridge with A.W. and Mills grenades.

No. **5 Keep** in the MARKET HALL. This will be the Home Guard Battle Headquarters and has a fair field of fire all round. Being such a high building look-outs on the roof can see the various other keeps, and snipers up there would dominate any enemy penetrating into the built-up part of the village. It is reasonably central and from it RESERVES could issue in any direction to reinforce threatened localities or to counter-attack in the event of a local success by the enemy.

Speed is essential in such operations, so the Reserve must always be placed in a central position.

The S.A.A. dump will be in No. 5 Keep and the position of this reserve ammunition should be known to all the N.C.Os.

13

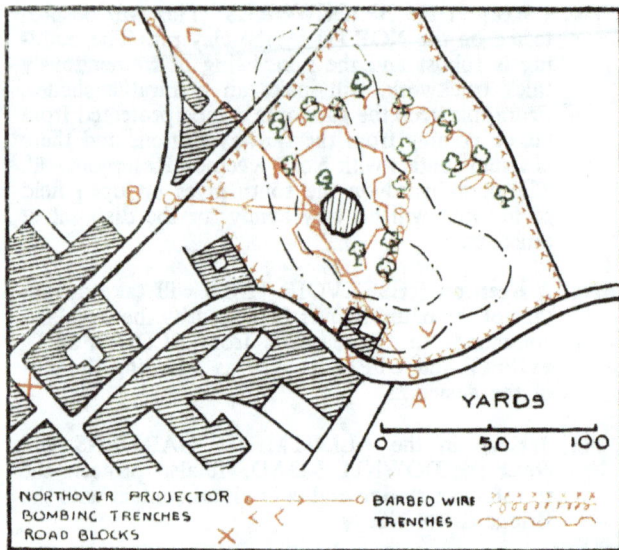

Legend:
- NORTHOVER PROJECTOR ●———→
- BOMBING TRENCHES < <
- ROAD BLOCKS ×
- BARBED WIRE
- TRENCHES

PLATE 4.—No. 2 KEEP

Note the wiring which follows hedges (or the side of the road) all round except a small stretch due west of the keep, which should go straight across so as to look like a fence or hedge. The trees are also laced together with wire.

The Northover projectors are on the near slope of the hill and cannot be seen or fired upon from the east. They cover the roads at A, B and C, and vehicles can be caused to hesitate at these spots by a cunning use of screens or dummy mines.

Bombers' trenches should be put within range of A, B and C so that once the Northovers set a tank alight Molotovs can be thrown to carry on the good work. These slit trenches should be well defiladed against a bad shot from the Northover, and great care should be taken to avoid making tracks.

14

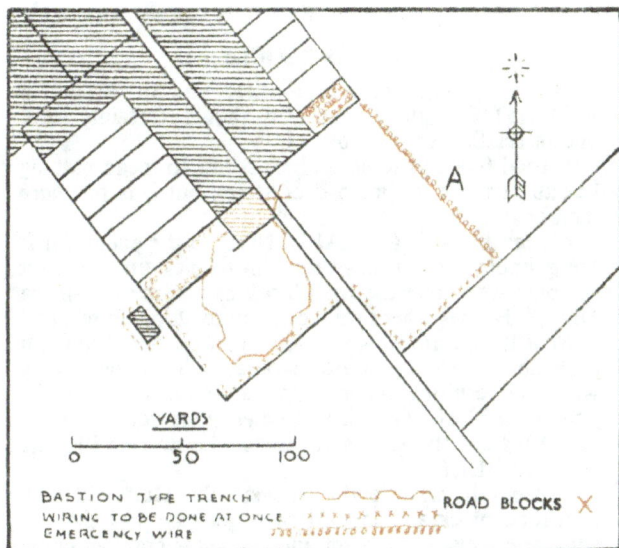

YARDS

| 0 | 50 | 100 |

BASTION TYPE TRENCH
WIRING TO BE DONE AT ONCE
EMERGENCY WIRE
ROAD BLOCKS X

PLATE 5.—No. 3 KEEP

A HOUSE has been included in this keep, as it dominates the road block and has a splendid field of fire.

The WIRING is along hedges and in two back gardens.

You will notice that some of the wiring comes much too close to the keep; but even so this is better than putting it farther out in the field, where it would be very obvious from the AIR.

A supply of Dannert wire should be kept ready for putting out at A (to look like a continuation of the garden fence) after the " balloon goes up."

Parts of the trench can be dug now to act as fire positions, and these may be connected up later if required.

The hedges should be cleared to give necessary field of fire, but with GREATEST DISCRIMINATION and care (and only low down at that).

15

V

ROAD BLOCKS

In my opening remarks I asked you to develop a REALISTIC outlook, and you should certainly have one in relation to road blocks.

A road block to some soldiers seems to mean nothing but an obstacle in the road or street, but it is *far more* than that.

A road block is a CHALLENGE to the enemy; it is the gauntlet thrown down for him to pick up. In effect the men who erect the road block say to the advancing Huns, " Here is where we mean you to stop. So what? "

Now if you are a wise soldier you do not throw out a challenge unless you are favourably fixed for dealing with the resulting schemozzle; consequently, you site your road block where it will be *easy* for you to defend and *hard* for the enemy to attack; because ATTACK IT HE WILL!

Those folk who fondly imagine the Hun will look at a road block and say, " I can't get past it; I shall go somewhere else," have got another guess coming, either in this world or in the next.

Surprise is a great factor in road-block tactics, but it is no use surprising your enemy unless you are in a position to take advantage of his temporary hesitation and confusion. In other words, if you place your road block where the hostile A.F.V. will come upon it suddenly and halt, you MUST have everything prepared to put him " on the spot " without a moment's delay.

When you think of putting a road block in a certain place, say to yourself, " What will the Boches do when they see a road block here? Will they try to get round the flanks? Which flank will they try first? Where shall I put some men to stop that? What about the other flank? What will he do if he cannot turn our flanks? Use a mortar? Where could the guard shelter? Where will they use a mortar from? How could we sneak out and ambush them there? "

And so on.

Having these considerations in mind, let us look at the map and fix some approximate positions for road blocks prior to reconnoitring them on the ground.

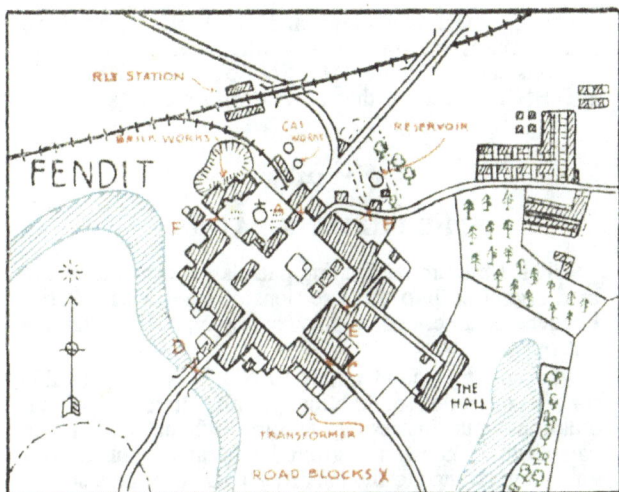

PLATE 6.—ROAD BLOCKS

Road Block A.—If we place a block just south of the gasworks it will block both the BLOODFORD and the POPPIT ROADS and we can put the guard in the gasworks, which will kill two birds with one stone. No. 2 Keep can also cover this road block.

Road Block B.—This should block the UPPIT ROAD and if it is put in the bend of the street it will be easy to defend from houses at both sides.

Road Block C.—This will stop any traffic from DOWN-IT and, being right up against No. 3 Keep, will require no special guard, but as it is on a straight road it will require screening carefully.

Road Block D on the bridge on the BEATIT ROAD is actually much easier to conceal than appears from the map, as the bridge has a high crown which will prevent an approaching vehicle from seeing it till on the centre of the bridge.

These four are the really hefty man's size road blocks required to deny the roads to the enemy.

Two other lighter road blocks will be an advantage, one where the drive from the Hall (E) enters the village and the other at the west corner of the churchyard (F).

17

Having fixed the keeps and road blocks we have formed the framework of the static defence, so now let us consider the more ACTIVE and AGGRESSIVE DEFENCE, because that is what *really* counts.

VI

THE FIGHTING PATROLS

When I talk about fighting patrols I mean twenty-five men organized into three sections of eight with a Patrol Leader, as described in my lecture on " The Fighting Patrol."

The country round about FENDIT is very suitable for the operation of fighting patrols. It is full of undulations and interesting features which will give a patrol which knows the ground a great advantage over an enemy strange to the locality. This advantage should be exploited by the Home Guard to the utmost, as it will largely offset the military training of the German invaders.

Now let us divide the surrounding district into fighting patrol areas. This is very necessary, because your fighting patrols should be trained to be very aggressive and swift to attack; consequently, if you have two of them out, particularly under conditions of bad visibility, etc., there is a risk of their attacking one another unless you tie them down to operating within certain specified boundaries.

These boundaries, by the way, should be well-marked geographical features, easily recognizable on the ground, such as streams, roads, woods, etc.

As apparently you will have only sufficient men to have two patrols out at once, what about dividing the surrounding district into two patrol areas, one south of the line made by the UPPIT—FENDIT ROAD as far as the bridge over the RIVER BOOZE south-west of FENDIT and thence along the BOOZE westwards, and the other north of it, the road itself to be inclusive to the southern patrol area?

Now for the OUTWARD limits of the patrol areas:

Fighting Patrol Operating from No. 2 Keep

NORTH WOOD stretches for two miles, so it is impossible to patrol the northern edge—that is, the BLOODFORD side; consequently, we have perforce to make our limit here from the RIVER BOOZE to the southern point and then along the edge of NORTH WOOD to POPPIT HOLLOW, which is big enough to hold an invading battalion without its being seen from the village, so it must be kept under continual observation.

From there POPPIT BROOK furnishes a good boundary till it strikes the UPPIT ROAD, which is the patrol's southern limit.

Fighting Patrol Operating from No. 3 Keep

This patrol is not so cramped in style and can cover more ground. From the UPPIT ROAD along LAD LANE to the INN, thence along SCRAM ROAD to the south side of PINE WOOD, along the southern edge of PINE and SOUTH WOODS, over the bridge along LASS LANE to BEATIT ROAD. Thence covering west edge of WEST WOOD, north along hedge to RIVER BOOZE. A lovely stretch of typical English countryside. If this patrol could be mounted on cycles they could cover their area so quickly and SILENTLY that they would be worth two or three unmounted patrols. Using the roads indicated on the map (at irregular times), they would be great protection to the main defences and sudden death to any small parties of enemy paratroops impudent enough to come down on their area. There are other ways of making patrols mobile besides cycles and these should all be considered. You see you will be short of men in this defence scheme (because everybody always *is* short of men in defence schemes!), and the fewer defenders you have the MORE ACTIVE THEY MUST BE!

Fighting Patrols from Neighbouring Villages

Plate 7 shows the two areas covered by fighting patrols from FENDIT. Do not forget that other villages within a mile or so will also send out patrols which in places will come right up to your boundaries. This means careful arrangements between you and the Officers Commanding adjoining Home Guard units.

Unless you make these arrangements now you may some time have a ghastly episode in which Home Guards kill each other.

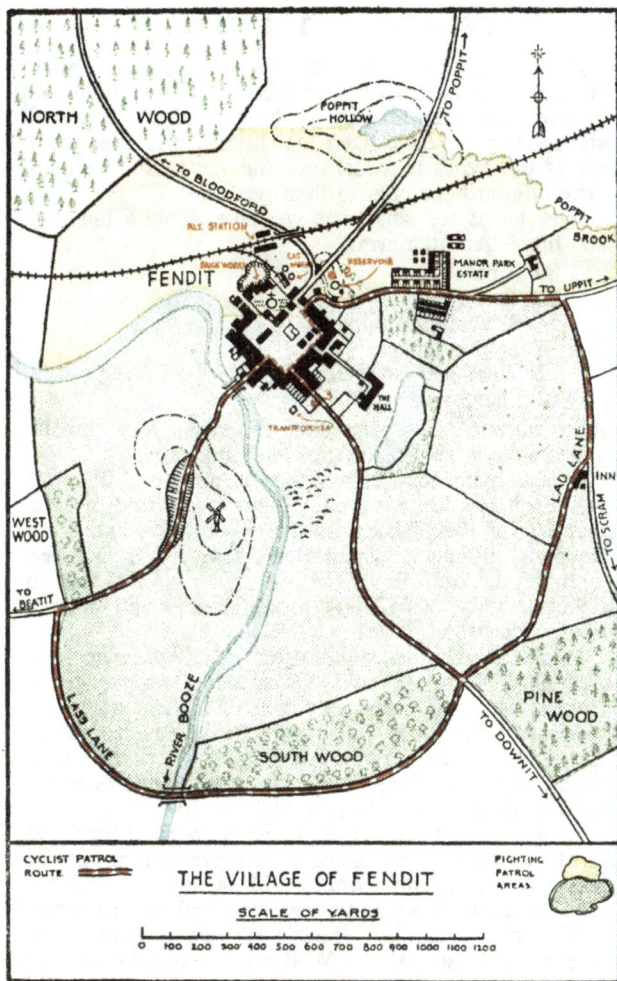

NORTH WOOD

TO POPPIT

POPPIT HOLLOW

TO BLOODFORD

POPPIT BROOK

RLY STATION

BRICK WORKS

GAS WORKS

RESERVOIR

MANOR PARK ESTATE

TO UPPIT

FENDIT

THE HALL

TRANSFORMER

LAD LANE

INN

TO SCRAM

WEST WOOD

TO BEATIT

PINE WOOD

LASS LANE

RIVER BOOZE

SOUTH WOOD

TO DOWNIT

CYCLIST PATROL ROUTE

FIGHTING PATROL AREAS

THE VILLAGE OF FENDIT

SCALE OF YARDS

0   100 200 300 400 500 600 700 800 900 1000 1100 1200

PLATE 7.—FIGHTING PATROLS

21

VII

THE MEN AND THE WEAPONS

We are getting on famously with our defensive arrangements now. We have sited the keeps, the backbone of our defence, and we have decided the patrol areas. Also we have fixed which particular keeps will act as the eyries to which our fighting patrols will return, like birds of prey to their nests.

Now let us see what men we have. Only a hundred and fifty! And the arms?

- 80 Rifles.
- 20 Shot-guns.
- 4 Browning automatics.
- 6 Tommy-guns.
- 2 Northover projectors.
- 2 Flame-throwers.

Also various Mills grenades, Molotovs, A.W. bombs and a few larger bombs and anti-tank mines.

Not as many men or weapons as we would like, but we might be a lot worse off. Anyway, it is said that the moral is to the physical as three is to one, and these weapons, although comparatively few, will, if handled with DASH and DETERMINATION, be sufficient to hold the village of FENDIT for a long time and to make the invader think twice.

What is the best allocation of these men and weapons? First the men. These are of various kinds, from quite young men to veterans of the last war.

Most of the latter will hardly be active enough for the fighting patrols, but are just the men to act as garrisons for the keeps while the more active ones are used as fighting patrols or mobile reserves.

If we allocate sixty men to garrison the keeps and have two fighting patrols of twenty-five men each, that leaves forty, of whom fifteen will be required as lookouts on road blocks and twenty-five will be in reserve.

The next point is: how shall we distribute the weapons? First the BROWNINGS. Probably the best place for these will be in Keeps Nos. 1, 2, 3 and 4. Of the TOMMY-GUNS let us put four in Keep No. 5 and give one to each FIGHTING PATROL.

Reasons for this are that Keep No. 5 has the shortest field of fire; also, should the enemy break into the village there will be house-to-house fighting for the reserves, who will find the tommy-guns just the tools required.

No. 2 Keep is a good spot for the NORTHOVER PROJECTORS, as from it they can strafe vehicles on three roads.

I should put the FLAME-THROWERS at Road Block B in the cellars of two houses so that they can poop off from ground level.

Distribute the bombs, etc., amongst the keeps and road-block guards, with some extra ones at No. 4 Keep.

As you have only a few ANTI-TANK MINES, they should be used to supplement the lighter Road Blocks E and F.

•

VIII

HOW WILL OUR DEFENCES WORK?

There you have your defence scheme. When the long-expected Huns approach the village of FENDIT they will be wondering what sort of a job you and I have made of the defence arrangements and hoping to surprise us.

The first indication of our activities will be when, without the least warning, a strong fighting patrol materializes from apparently nowhere and rushes in on them, yelling like fiends so suddenly that before they can do anything they feel the cold steel enter their vitals and realize too late that the soil they came to conquer they will remain to fertilize.

After that may come other much stronger bodies of the enemy, so strong that the fighting patrols cannot tackle them, but will have to retire to their keeps section by section, each giving the other covering fire.

Following the retiring patrols as closely as they dare, the Germans will come suddenly under close and accurate fire from the keeps, not one of which has fired a shot at long range, but has simply lain doggo waiting for the enemy to get so close that every shot will tell.

Then there will be a lull while the Nazis study our defences with glasses, make their plans and possibly bring up some mortars and machine guns.

The battle will then commence in real earnest and two or three of the keeps may be attacked at once while parties of Germans will push forward, trying to find a weak spot. One party may make the mistake of approaching a keep in too weak strength and find to its cost that the garrison do not wait to be attacked, but rush out and get the first smack in.

Some of the enemy may even penetrate past the road blocks into the village, only to find that the reserves issue from Keep No. 5 and, dodging round familiar entries and side streets, bump them off from their flanks and rear; even from roofs and windows, piling up the blood-stained grey corpses all over the place.

After this has gone on for a while the German Commander (if still living) will suddenly say " Heil, Hitler! I've had enough of this goddam bloody place : we'll take what men are left and see what we can do at POPPIT ! "

As they slink away and the fighting patrols are emerging from the keeps to harass their withdrawal, they will know the answer to their original question about the defences of FENDIT.

IX

ROUNDING OFF THE DEFENCE SCHEME

Now, having done the bulk of the work, let us round off our defence scheme by attending to a number of points which must not be overlooked if we are to complete a workmanlike job.

THE IMPORTANCE OF THE TIME FACTOR

It is not generally realized how vastly important the time factor is in modern mechanized warfare, when mobile and armoured units are manœuvring for position.

A check given to the head of a column proceeding across country will be magnified many times over. Consequently, one village stubbornly denying the enemy's passage may give our own units time to arrive at the tactical point and so influence a tremendous battle.

This I would impress upon you most emphatically so that you can make absolutely clear to your men that, although the situation may appear desperate and hopeless, it is still of use to FIGHT ON.

If every town and village in the country realizes this and, when the invader comes, fights and fights and FIGHTS, the result of their combined efforts will be *decisive*.

LIAISE WITH CIVIL AUTHORITIES

Keep close touch with the head of the local Council, the Police and the A.R.P. Services, as well as the heads of the Electricity, Gas and Water Services. All these have a direct bearing on defensive measures. Remember, if your Home Guard comes into action you will be dependent on the CIVIL arrangements for the care of your wounded. Make friends with the W.V.S.: they will cook, provide comforts and do all sorts of things for your men. In war they will be an invaluable aid if you will enlist their interest and help now.

Get to know about FOOD supplies in the village. What they are, where they are, and who looks after them. Should the state of tension last some time you may be very glad of this information. Establish close touch with neighbouring military and other units. Get to know their plans and co-ordinate your arrangements.

Acquaint yourself with the arrangements for preventing PETROL falling into the enemy's hands, and as there are some large, flat fields, see that they are obstructed with stout posts, etc., because, good though your defence scheme may be, it is no use *inviting* attack.

BARBED WIRE

See about plenty of entanglements, but always keep them under cover, along hedges, in ditches, etc. The enemy will probably do FENDIT the honour of taking its photograph, and irresponsible wiring will tell him exactly where you intend to put your men. Coiled Dannert wire should be distributed in various places ready to be rushed out on emergency.

The details of R.E. and other stores required, together with instruction in the building of defence works, siting of trenches, reinforcing of houses, etc., form too varied a subject to be dealt with here; so I have treated them separately.

COMMUNICATIONS

You may have very little signalling equipment, but do not worry about that. Amongst your men will be some old signallers: start them practising at once and fix up flag and lamp communications between important points. Be sure that all ranks have plenty of practice in sending information quickly and accurately. Study means of communication between yourself and neighbouring units.

TANK TRAPS

A few TANK TRAPS will be most useful and give everyone a great sense of security. Pits covered over, streams cunningly deepened, and all kinds of obstacles can be devised without a tremendous lot of work.

The construction of these highly interesting aids to defence, as well as booby-traps of various kinds, I have dealt with elsewhere.

WATER

Water can often be utilized for defensive purposes; for instance, it appears from the map that it would be easy to partially dam the RIVER BOOZE at WINDMILL HILL and so flood the marsh up to the lake. This would make the south side of the village very secure. Also it may be possible to use boats to patrol the river or to move reserves to surprise the enemy.

SHOT-GUNS

I have noticed a tendency amongst the Home Guard to disparage shot-guns in favour of rifles. This is a big mistake: a shot-gun in the hands of one accustomed to using it, firing buckshot, is deadlier than a rifle at short range, and ALL the shooting, whether by rifles or shot-guns, SHOULD BE AT SHORT RANGES.

TRAINING

Having decided on your defensive arrangements, the next thing is to train your men to carry them out efficiently. The training of fighting patrols is of endless interest and can be varied in lots of ways.

House-to-house fighting is a study in itself and practice is absolutely essential if you are to avoid casualties and kill the invaders.

Train your men to shoot accurately at close ranges both in daylight and DARKNESS.

CHRONOLOGICAL DEFENCE IN DEPTH

And now, before we come to the end of what I feel has been a very sketchy outline of a complex subject, I should like to say a few words about something which has been on my mind lately: —

We hear a lot about defence in depth and everyone agrees that it is the essential thing, but they all mean depth in the GEOGRAPHICAL sense—that is, depth in terms of yards and miles.

I want to talk about depth in the CHRONOLOGICAL sense—I mean DEPTH IN TIME, in days and weeks.

Suppose that in spite of our preparations and all the valiant work of the FENDIT Home Guard, the enemy brings up more and more men, breaks down the defences and occupies the village.

Is *that* going to be the *end* of the resistance put up by the FENDIT people?

Or are some of the hardy spirits amongst the villagers going to carry on the war against the uninvited guests every day, and particularly every night, WEEK IN, WEEK OUT?

I'll say they are!

There will be many a splash in the waters of the River Booze when sentries disappear on dark nights. There will be unexpected stabbings and shootings and fires and explosions galore till the enemy's nerves are all awry and he gets increasingly powerless to hold the place.

But, in order to do this successfully, preparations should be made *before* the occupation. Little stores of weapons, clothes, explosives and food should be carefully hidden here and there, safe from the damp and the rats. These should be known to a very few selected men and the utmost secrecy observed.

Still, that is all by the way, and if your defence is properly carried out it is unlikely to arise.

So now for my last word. In all your preparations to repel the invader put yourself into his place. Use your imagination and say, " What will he do? How will he do it? " and the answers will never fail to give you the clue to a SUCCESSFUL DEFENCE.

www.ingramcontent.com/pod-product-compliance
Lightning Source LLC
LaVergne TN
LVHW021130080426
835511LV00010B/1812